LET'S LOOK AT
Kitchen

Nicola Tuxworth

LORENZ BOOKS

Plates and things

Glasses, bowls and plates are often kept in the cupboard.

four soup bowls

four shiny mugs

four dinner plates

four colored
glasses

creamer

fat teapot

pitcher

vegetable dish

Let's put these
things away.

Dried foods

These foods can be kept for a long time.

white flour

kidney beans

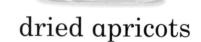
dried apricots

red lentils

white rice

pasta

coffee
beans

crunchy cookies

tea

Just one more
cookie, while
Mom's not
looking!

spaghetti

raisins

Cans, jars and bottles

Some food goes in special containers.

cherries in syrup

tuna

ketchup

apricot jam

apple juice

tomato soup

olive oil

honey

sunflower
oil

crunchy peanut
butter

I'm having jam
on my toast ...

... I hope!

In the refrigerator

Some food needs to be kept cold to stay fresh.

silver
sardines

salted
butter

roast chicken

milk

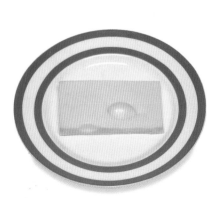

Swiss cheese

I'm drinking
cold milk.

In the freezer

Some foods have to be kept frozen.

fish sticks

crazy ice shapes

orange popsicles

tiny green peas

crinkly French fries

Fruit and vegetables

Do you know what these fruits and vegetables are called?

broccoli

grapefruit

kiwi fruit

onions

black grapes

bananas

potatoes

zucchini

oranges

apples

Which fruit shall I have?

Machines and gadgets

The kitchen is full of things to help you do a job more easily.

colander

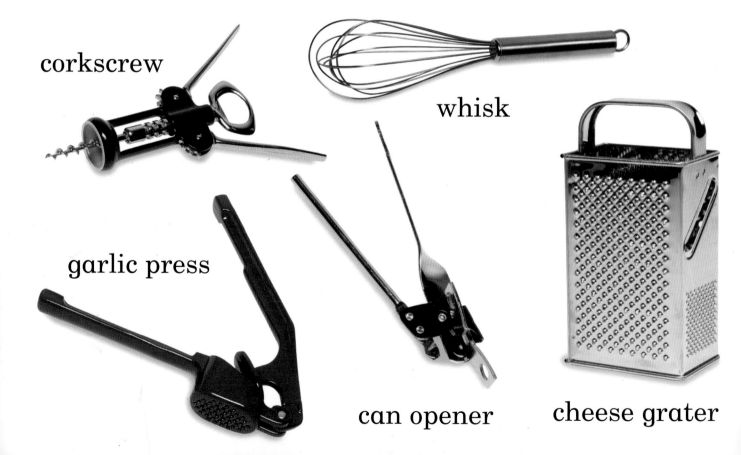

corkscrew

whisk

garlic press

can opener

cheese grater

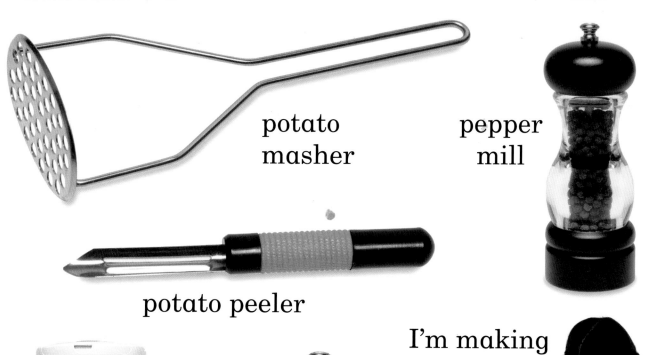

potato
masher

pepper
mill

potato peeler

I'm making
pancakes.

salt
mill

blender

Let's cook!

There are lots of special things to cook with in the kitchen.

wooden spoons

oven mitt

wire cake rack

casserole

frying pan

spatula

saucepan

slotted
spoon

ladle

cake
pans

Mmm, delicious!

What's for lunch?

We often eat our meals in the kitchen.

I'm setting the table.

place mats

forks

teaspoons

knives

dessert spoons

napkins

orange juice

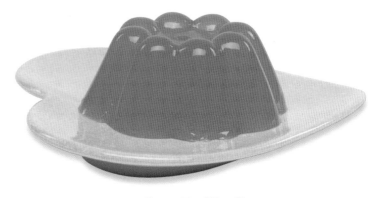

jiggly Jell-O

spaghetti
with tomato
sauce

plastic glasses

It's fun to
have a
friend
to lunch.

Cleaning up

There are lots of
things to help us
clean up in
the kitchen.

feather
duster

bucket

Almost
finished!

sponge

mop

pot
scourer

dishpan

washcloth

dishwashing liquid

dustpan and brush

brush

I like mopping the floor best!

dish towel

broom

What is it for?

Do you know what these kitchen things are for?